R[illegible]
WORD

Also by Fraser Keay

The Abuse of Power and the Grace of God
(e-book and audiobook)

The Character and Timing
of the Kingdom of God
(e-book)

The King's Table
(e-book and audiobook)

Youth Ministry Across the Continents:
Eleven Youth Pastors from Ten Countries on
the Key Building Blocks for Effective Youth
Work Leadership in the Local Church
(paperback, 2nd edition)

Mentoring Ministry:
How God Can Use You to Shape the Following
Generations
(e-book, paperback and audiobook)

Fighter, Fugitive, King:
David's Leadership Development, How
it Can Point Men to Christ,
and its Relevance Today
(e-book, paperback, hardback and audiobook)

THE RHEMA WORD

ITS MEANING, MISUSE AND PURPOSE

FRASER KEAY

ILLUMINE PRESS

The Rhema Word: Its Meaning, Misuse and Purpose

Published by Illumine Press, an imprint of
First Half Leadership Publishing,
United Kingdom

ISBN: 979-8-7678956-8-7 (paperback)

ISBN: 978-0-9954729-5-2 (e-book)

Email address for all publishing matters:

firsthalfleadership@gmail.com

For Jonny and Dade, in appreciation of many stimulating conversations

CONTENTS

INTRODUCTION

There is a little bit of confusion in some circles about the Greek words *logos* and *rhema* and what they mean in the New Testament. Some believers, especially in charismatic circles, can end up sitting with their Bibles in front of them waiting for a *rhema* word when they actually need to better learn how to pick up their knife and fork and dig into the Bible, use their mind, consider the context of the verse they are looking at, while asking God for *illumination*, for him to shine his light on the Scriptures they are reading or listening to. I believe that part of this problem comes from confusing teaching with prophecy and how they both work.

God can and does highlight things in Scripture to us, illuminate, shine his divine light on his written word, as well as bring specific verses to mind when we need them, but the word of God does not change into a 'rhema' word, a personal 'now' word to us,[1] 'a word that has become revelation'.[2] The *rhema* is not hidden within the *logos*.

The aim of this short book is to help you gain some knowledge about the difference between *logos* and *rhema*, appreciate the importance of context when it comes to words, better distinguish between *illumination* and receiving a *revelation*, and give you a couple of alternative language tools that better serve to explain the amazing ways that God speaks to people through his Spirit and in his word, the Scriptures.

This book is adapted from one of the appendices in the book, *Fighter, Fugitive, King: David's Leadership Development, How it Can Point Men to Christ, and its Relevance Today (2021).*

CHAPTER 1

The difference between teaching and a revelation

A 'teaching' (Greek didache) and a 'revelation' (Greek apokalupto) are clearly distinguished in 1 Corinthians 14:26. They involve us using different faculties.

1. Being given an understanding about some Scripture or bringing a *teaching* involves first being given 'illumination': God shining his light on our hearts so we can grasp, perceive, comprehend the truth of what we are reading or hearing in the inspired and living Word of God. The word *illumination* comes from a Greek word ('*photizo*' – the root Greek word is '*phos*' from which we get 'light' and 'photo') meaning 'to illumine, to light up'. It is used in John 1:9 'the true *light* that gives light to everyone' (my italics). Jesus did it directly with the two on the road to Emmaus, opening up the Scriptures to them (Luke 24:13-35).

An Old Testament verse carrying the same idea is Psalm 119:18, 'Open my eyes, that I might see wonderful things in your law'. It's the clear acknowledgement and prayer that we need God the Holy Spirit to give us spiritual understanding as we read or listen to the Word of God. It's when God shines his light on the eyes of our heart, provides insight, opens our eyes. It's as if someone turns on the lights in a dark room; suddenly, we can see! For some, like Paul, who studied the Old Testament in depth for years before he could see spiritually, it's like the lights being turned on *in a library*. Same with the noted teacher Apollos who really knew the Old Testament (Acts 18). They have much to go over, much to re-examine. It's little wonder some people end up in some backwater or isolated situation for a long period – necessary time to review and reconsider the Scriptures they know so well or revise preconceived notions about the faith.

Paul wrote to Timothy, 'Reflect on what I am saying, for the Lord will give you insight into all this,' i.e. gain understanding as he reflected on Paul's words, which were to become part of holy Scripture (2 Timothy 2:7). That word translated 'insight' is also used by Paul when writing to the Ephesians, that they would read his letter so that they could understand his 'insight' into the mystery of Christ – that the Gentiles would join the Jews as heirs in Christ (Ephesians 3:4-6). It means 'putting things together' in their understanding; in other words, piecing it all together, getting the picture, 'joining the dots' as we might say. It's when we're reading or listening to something in Scripture, something we may have read or heard many times before, and suddenly we 'get it'.

When this happens for the very first time, a veil over our heart is removed: we see the light of the gospel that displays the glory of Christ, turning to him. We see who Jesus is, turning from our sin, putting our faith in him. Which is also why preaching is so important (2 Corinthians 3:12 – 4:6). And it's not simply a matter of grammar, or mental prowess, although the words of course need to make sense to us, and not confuse us. If it were purely about grammar etc, then experts in the languages the Bible was originally written in would be the closest to God.

2. Being given a *revelation* (noun), for example a dream or vision or some other way of God speaking directly to us, such as a gentle whisper, a light or cloud and a voice from heaven, or even a trance (see 1 Kings 19:12, Matthew 1:20, Luke 1:22, Luke 9:28-36, Acts 8:26-40, 9:1-10 & 10:10) does *not* come as a result of applying our minds as we study Scripture and asking God for *illumination*. It's something we *receive in our spirit* and which sometimes affects our whole being (consider the biblical examples above).

I have a friend to whose bedroom window God sent a ball of light in the middle of the night. He experienced a tremendous sense of the Lord's presence as he hid under the bed covers. As he had been becoming more conscious of God's presence over the weeks he was very aware it was a heavenly visitation of some sort (we might recall that 'a light from heaven flashed around Paul' – Acts 9:3 – so there is a direct precedent). There were no lampposts or other lights outside his window. He's also a scientist by profession and so less likely than some to get carried away by something unusual. It was no deceiving angel. He came to faith not long afterwards and has been following Jesus for the last 35 years.

A *revelation* is also something we may then share *if we sense permission from God to do so* (Matthew 17:9). In the same way, the spirit of those who prophesy is also under their control: it's not a case of hysteria or 'I just had to speak that out, I couldn't help it' (i.e. no self control). God is a God of order, but not lacking power or desire to equip churches with lots of spiritual gifts (1 Corinthians 1:7; and 1 Corinthians 14, especially verse 32). For example, we receive a revelation and then later share it; when we share it, it is a prophecy, a spoken or written report to the other person or people, something uttered for the benefit of others.

An excellent Old Testament example of this process is Nathan receiving a revelation and then reporting it to King David (2 Samuel 7). The revelation didn't come to David; it came to Nathan, who then shared it with David. To David it was a prophecy, a prophetic word. Paul speaks about this exact same process in 1 Corinthians chapter 14:26-32 in respect of a church gathering. A *revelation* is spontaneously received by someone 'sitting down' among the gathered congregation, i.e. the person is not standing up and speaking aloud at that time for all present to hear.

But when and if they do speak out, i.e. share that revelation, it's then a prophecy – a report of what they sense God has revealed to them for the benefit of others in the congregation. The congregation can then weigh up, test, judge that report (1 Corinthians 14:29; 1 Thessalonians 5:19-22).

It's when we distinctly sense that God has spoken to us somehow, given us a *revelation* about something *apart from* when we are studying the Bible. Which is why it can happen anywhere. Reflect for a moment on *where* people were or what they were doing in the various biblical examples we have about someone receiving a revelation. It's as if God is 'pulling back the curtain' on something for us to see, revealing something to us that we would not otherwise know. Another useful image is that of 'being given a song', of having something suddenly come to us (for which we would use a plectrum / pick if we think of the image of playing a guitar). To underline the difference between a teaching (for which, like Bible study, we need *illumination*) and a prophecy etc (for which first we need a *revelation*), again consider the biblical examples already mentioned. Did Joseph have a dream in response to his request to better understand a Scripture? Did Zechariah have a vision of an angel as he pored over some Scripture, asking for illumination? Did an angel speak to Philip (the evangelist) to give him understanding about some passage of Scripture he was considering? Did Peter fall into a Spirit-induced trance in response to his focused reading of something in the Law or the Prophets? Did Nathan receive a revelation in the middle of the night to help him explain some Scripture or other? The answer to all these questions is no. What is recorded for us in all these instances is the process of being given a *revelation* by the Holy Spirit.

In Acts 10 we read of Peter receiving a *revelation* that will have completely changed his view of Scripture, especially the right use of the Law of Moses. But it was a *revelation*, a dramatic starting point on a journey to help him realise that God accepts people from every nation. God graciously and powerfully built on this revelation by telling him to then go with some seemingly random men who had just arrived at the place he was staying at, and go with them to see the unconverted Roman soldier Cornelius, to whom God had also given a revelation. God then flooded that gathering of Gentiles at Cornelius' house with his Spirit, interrupting Peter's preaching. Which should also tell us that it was not only a historically important moment in the development of the Church in accepting Gentiles, it was the outworking of God's plan to bless all nations, and an example of God's promise to pour out his Spirit on all in the last days – the time from Jesus' ascension *to his return* – and that God is quite willing to interrupt our meetings by the influence of his Spirit and introduce other gifts into the mix, yet without minimising the importance of evangelistic preaching.

God very well might reveal something specific to someone to share *apart from* or *in addition to* their study of the Bible or indeed their preaching, but in that instance it would be teaching with, e.g. prophecy added in; teaching with some other word or other added. It's a *revelation* God has given the person *in addition to* the *teaching* they brought, the sermon they preached, the message they shared (usually with a fair amount of study with *illumination* beforehand). It's the same God, the same Holy Spirit at work revealing things to the person, but one is a *teaching* (for which we first need *illumination*), the other a *revelation*. Two different things. I hope I'm making this clear. Daniel 9:2 and 10:1 are also instructive in this matter in terms of distinguishing between on the one hand being given understanding about some Scripture or some teaching from Scripture (9:2), and a revelation on the other hand (10:1).

Yes, both are aspects of God revealing things to us, but one is more to with the mind (being given *illumination* as we study the Scriptures, from which someone gifted to teach may share 'a teaching'), the other more to do with receiving something in our spirit (a *revelation*).

CHAPTER 2

Logos and rhema

The argument for logos meaning the whole of Scripture or the written word of God, and rhema being an inspired, specific, spoken word from within it, can be traced back to the book, From the Pinnacle of the Temple (1979) by Charles Farah. There may be another earlier development someone knows of.

Farah may have leaned on William Vine's *Expository Dictionary of New Testament Words* first published in 1940. It was for many years a helpful resource, especially for those who hadn't studied any of the biblical languages. It states, 'The significance of *rhema* (as distinct from *logos*), is exemplified in the injunction to take 'the sword of the Spirit, which is the word of God' (Ephesians 6:17); here the reference is not to the whole Bible as such, but to the individual scripture which the Spirit brings to our remembrance for use in time of need, a prerequisite being the regular storing of the mind with Scripture.'[3]

Farah argues that the *logos-rhema* distinction is a theological construct, i.e. a tool or device to help us better understand and communicate matters about the faith. He states that the apostle John often uses *logos* to mean the universal and eternal, the word of God, i.e. Christ (e.g. John 1:1 and 1:14). And since *rhema* is sometimes used to mean a 'now' word, a personal word for the moment, a spoken word for a specific person, if you contrast *logos* and *rhema* then you can use it as 'a teaching tool that helps us to understand *the difference between a general and a particular word of the Lord*' (my emphasis).[4] But as Farah readily admits, 'the Scriptures...do not teach a clear and unambiguous distinction between these two words.'[5] He states that the two words are used interchangeably in the Bible, 'except in John'.[6] The problem is, that is simply incorrect: they are used interchangeably in John as well, with a couple of notable uses at the start of John that point to the deity of our wonderful Saviour.

1. *Logos* (pronounced in the original, 'log-os') appears over 300 times in the New Testament and can be used to describe someone speaking (a speech or a report or a statement), or an idea or reasoning expressed by words. It can also be used in a weighty theological sense, depending on the context, as in John 1:1 and 1:14 (the *logos*, the pre-existing Word became flesh).

Logos is also used by the woman at the well in her 'testimony' (the 'logon' [from *logos*] of the woman) afterwards to her village. It was her spoken word, her testimony, her report (John 4:39). Jesus healed an official's son simply by uttering a word. He said, 'Go, your son will live' (4:50), it states that the man believed the specific 'word' Jesus spoke to him. And the Greek used in that sentence? *Logos,* not *rhema.* You might argue that this is the written record, the Scriptures, so these examples and Jesus' words are all *logos,* not *rhema.* But as we'll see, from the Bible you cannot argue that *logos* equals the written word of God, and that *rhema* equals the spoken or inspired word of God.

When Jesus was in Jerusalem teaching, some Jews asked: "What did he mean (literally, 'what is the "word" – the *logos*') when he said, 'You will look for me, but you will not find me'" (John 7:36). In other words, 'What did Jesus mean by the things (the *logos*) he said?'

Of importance is John 12:48 where both *logos* and *rhema* are used very close to each other: 'There is a judge for the one who rejects me and does not accept my words (*rhema*); the very words (*logos*) I have spoken will condemn them at the last day.'

Finally, consider the specific spoken words by the Jewish leaders to Pilate: 'If you let this man go, you are no friend of Caesar. Anyone who claims to be a king opposes Caesar' (John 19:12). 'When Pilate heard 'this' (logon [plural of *logos*], i.e. the words of the Jewish leaders), he brought Jesus out' (John 19:13). Pilate was referring to the specific spoken words of the Jewish leaders.

As importantly, while *logos* is used in John 1:1, 14 and Revelation 19:13 to refer to Jesus the 'Word of God', it is not used in the New Testament to define 'the Scriptures', i.e. the written word of God. A different word is used for that (see the section further on *The written word of God.)* As we've seen, *logos* has a wide range of usage, including referring to the word of God, from which we can sometimes take to mean the Scriptures. For example, Jesus said, 'If he called them "gods," to whom the word of God (the logos of God) came – and the Scripture cannot be set aside – what about the one, etc... (John 10:35). Jesus often said, 'It is written' and 'Have you never read?' by which he was of course referring to the Old Testament writings (Luke 24:44). He said he had come to 'fulfil the law'. The eternal and living Word of God, the Lord Jesus, came to fulfil the writings, the written word of God. Hallelujah. Jesus quoted a Scripture (in Isaiah 29) when he told some Pharisees, 'You have let go of the commands of God and are holding onto human traditions' (Mark 7:8).

As Farah rightly points out, *logos* is used by other New Testament writers in a variety of ways. Consider Paul's letter to the Ephesians: 'Do not let any unwholesome talk (*logos*) come out of your mouths' (4:29), and 'Pray also for me, that whenever I speak, words (*logos*) may be given me so that I will fearlessly make known the mystery of the gospel' (6:19). In Acts, *logos* often refers to the gospel (the 'word of the Lord' or 'the word of God') but it's also used in other situations, e.g. Ananias fell down dead when he heard Peter's 'words' (Acts 5:5), 'logos' in plural. Some of us would have definitely said that that was a *rhema* word, a now or special word Peter had for Ananias. But the word used is *logos*, and more importantly it does not carry any weight in the sentence, i.e. it's not central to understanding the sentence or passage. It's the *content* of his words that were important. And consider the word used for 'the word/message of wisdom' and 'the word/message of knowledge', both spiritual gifts involving people *speaking* out something God has revealed to them (1 Corinthians 12:8). You guessed it: *logos*.

As with John 12:48, we see *logos* and *rhema* being used by Peter in his first letter to refer to 'the word of God' and 'the word of the Lord'. The end of 1 Peter chapter 1: 'For you have been born again, not of perishable seed, but of imperishable, through the living and enduring word (*logos*) of God. For "All people are like grass...but the word (*rhema*) of the Lord endures forever." And this was the word (*rhema*) that was preached to you' (1 Peter 1:23-25). Peter was not referring to some specific *rhema* word he took from the written *logos* of God (in his context the Old Testament) because a. He uses *rhema* to refer to the enduring *word* of the Lord (the same word for 'enduring' or 'abiding' is also used before the enduring *logos* of God, i.e. one and same thing); and b. He was writing to believers scattered across hundreds of square miles. There's no evidence to suggest that by 'this was the *rhema* that was preached to you' he was referring to some specific spoken sermon they had all heard. He was using *logos* and *rhema* interchangeably to refer to the enduring 'word of God' or 'word of the Lord'.

2. *Rhema* (pronounced in the original 'ray-mah') appears 70 times in the New Testament and means a thing spoken, a word or saying of any kind, quite often a specific word or utterance; or words about an event or thing or object (as in 2 Corinthians 13:1). It is never used to refer to some special word of revelation. As we've seen, and as Vine above says, *rhema* is indeed used to describe the sword of the Spirit, i.e. the word of God (Ephesians 6:17). And 'every word (*rhema*) that comes from the mouth of God' (Matthew 4:4). But not only is *rhema* used to refer to specific human speech, especially by people, it is also sometimes used to mean the more general, which a saying or expression of any kind must necessarily include. For example, Jesus said, "Whoever belongs to God hears what God 'says' (his words – *rhema*) ..." (John 8:47). Are we going to argue that Jesus was excluding the Scriptures in that sentence or context, or by *rhema* he was referring to some specific words from Scripture or 'now' words that are inspired and that the Scriptures are not? Peter exclaimed, "You [Jesus] have the 'words' (*rhema* in plural) of eternal life!" (John 6:68). Referring to the Church, Paul wrote, "...to make her holy, cleansing her by the washing with water through the 'word' " (again, from *rhema*) (Ephesians 5:26).

What Paul is getting at in Ephesians

6:17 by the 'the sword of the Spirit', and what's recorded for us in Matthew 4 is quoting the word of God *as a sword* – three examples in Matthew 4 about *speaking out* words, Bible verses, to quickly rebut Satan. Christ is our example. We are commanded to do the same by memorising Scripture (Psalm 119:11) and trusting that the Holy Spirit will bring those words to mind, shine his light on specific words of Scripture which will then help us defeat Satan, and also sin, especially during trials in which we not only need perseverance but wisdom. God is unchanging and good and not a deceiver (read James 1:1-18). It's all part of submitting to God and resisting the devil (James 4:7), which when put in context of the surrounding verses in James 4 involves us not being friends with the world by arguing with each other because we selfishly want this and that from God so we can spend money on our pleasures. If we try and resist the devil when we are not submitted to God, we will soon fall flat on our faces or get horribly exposed to the enemy who can see clearly that we have no authority due to not being under authority. The order is submission to God, then resisting the devil.

I was once in a small group of young people who had pulled away from the main gathering at a youth retreat late one evening. Some of those present started rebuking the devil. One of them suddenly began to get suffocated, gasping for breath; it was like an invisible hand had grabbed her by the throat. It did not take a genius to work out that an evil spirit had been permitted to harass or oppress her. A few little lambs had left the safety of the flock and had decided to shout abuse at the wolves encircling the field. A more experienced believer, a woman, then came into the room, and gently placing one hand on the young woman's throat simply said, 'Satan, I bind you in Jesus' name.' She was immediately released, letting out a gasp of air. At the time it was short but very dramatic. We were ordered to get to bed, which we happily did. And we had all learned an important lesson.

In Ephesians, Paul was using the image of the Roman soldier to illustrate the cutting and thrusting edge of the sharpness of God's word. It is not only effective against sin and the Tempter, it also cuts to the heart, divides between soul and spirit. The *logos* of God is alive and active and exposes the thoughts and attitudes of the human heart (Hebrews 4:12). When we hear his voice, God speaking to us as we read Scriptures, or in some other way, we are not to harden our hearts but instead combine our hearing with faith: believe and obey God and not be like those who fell in the desert (Hebrews 3:1 – 4:13).

CHAPTER 3

A problem for some, not for others

In conservative evangelical churches none of this is really an issue, as it's not the language of faith they use to describe such things. And if you don't know any Greek then it may not be an issue. At the same time, those who have studied Greek may cringe when they hear blanket statements about logos and rhema as they double check their Greek New Testament and think, 'Mmm, that's not true'.

So what's going on?

People often appreciate hooks to hang things on. Farah is arguing for a *logos-rhema* distinction and using it as a theological tool, language that may help us better understand and explain spiritual matters, when something we've read in Scripture becomes fresh to us or is brought to mind by the Spirit. But as Farah clearly agrees, the use of both *logos* and *rhema* in the New Testament depends on the immediate context, which is why they are used in a variety of ways. Same with any word. For example, think of the different meanings the word 'trunk' might have when talking about driving a family *car* (UK - boot) on a safari surrounded by *trees* and *elephants* – three different possible trunks. As we've seen, John does use *logos* to refer to Christ, the pre-existent Word, in his account of the gospel (John 1:1 and 1:14) but forging a New Testament theological tool on the basis of how one word is *sometimes* used in a single book of the Bible may cause trouble for some people further down the line. Even if it was often used that way it's still fraught with danger.

It may help people not to jump to conclusions when they read something written in the Bible, as in the classic case of a new believer reading in one scripture 'Judas hanged himself' (Matthew 23:5) and then the next 'Now that you know these things, you will be blessed if you do them' (John 13:17) and then wondering if he/she should end it all (or jump off a cliff as Satan tempted Jesus with when misquoting Psalm 91 – Luke 4:10).

But we don't need a *logos-rhema* tool to tell us that this is just wrong; we need divine *illumination* as we read, God's flashlight/torch on our thinking, a growing knowledge of the breadth of God's Word, memorising it, so that we can recognise misquotes for what they really are: deception, or ignorance.

Jesus cited three specific verses from Deuteronomy in his encounter with the Tempter in the desert (Matthew 4). There were no shortcuts: in his humanity, Jesus will have memorised these. It's the same for us. As we do this, being in submission to God, the Holy Spirit will graciously bring to mind specific Scriptures when we most need them; he will teach and remind us of the things God has spoken to us before (John 14:26).

Farah claims that using *logos-rhema* does not need 'complete scriptural endorsement.'[7] But you can't build a trustworthy tool by using two words in the Bible to mean something when it does not fit with how those words are used in the Bible. That tool can eventually become an unreliable instrument, especially in immature, or worse, deceptive hands. Farah does offer a word of caution,[8] stating that the tool is not a doctrine. But in some circles, it has become just that. Ironically, a good number of teachers, including those in the 'word of faith' movement whose teaching Farah was challenging in the same book, have used his *logos-rhema* tool to promote their doctrines, confusing 'teaching' with 'revelation,' using the *rhema* argument to claim biblical verses mean something the context does not teach.

CHAPTER 4

Farah's motive

Farah was trying to explain why some people had not been physically healed. Some people had wrongly taken for themselves some words spoken that were actually intended for others, i.e. the word received or believed, or that had been preached or shared, had been a rhema word, a 'now word', but it was for someone else, not them. It became rhema for the other person but remained logos for them. 'Confession', was not, after all, 'possession'; while encouraging greater faith, you couldn't just 'name and claim it.'

For example, he uses the story of Jesus' interaction with John and Peter in John 21 to emphasise his point. He argues that

Jesus was saying in his reply to Peter when Peter asked, 'What about him?' (i.e. John): 'I have a *rhema* for you, and I have *rhema* for John, but the *rhema* I have for John is none of your business'.[9] The word *rhema* is not anywhere in that passage, and the word *logos* is used to describe the rumour, the 'words' the *disciples* used about the matter afterwards.

As a tool, *logos* vs. *rhema can* be used to illustrate that Jesus' words to someone else are not really any of our business: we must follow him. *But we don't need logos vs rhema to try and explain that: the context tells us* (some sanctified common sense doesn't hurt either in some instances.)

As mentioned, Farah relies largely on the gospel according to John for his *logos-rhema* distinction argument and tool, and I appreciate his heart in seeking to combat some of the excesses in the charismatic movement he was seeing at the time (and which still exist), and the pain caused – he dedicates the book to those 'for whom a faith-formula has not worked'). But in trying to explain what went wrong he has perhaps created a tool some teachers have since gone on to make an important doctrine. Some have even added it to their list of doctrines that helps earn them lots of money (prosperity teaching / the prosperity gospel).

The biblical use of both *logos* and *rhema* (especially in John 12:48 and 1 Peter 1:23-25) only underlines the fact that we cannot neatly divide the words up to create a solid theological tool, as attractive or as helpful that seems, because it is not consistent with Scripture itself. And it's so easily distorted. *Rhema* can end up topping *logos*: a so-called 'revelation' can supersede the plain meaning of the biblical text in front of us, especially if the person does not know their Bible. It may be a helpful illustration, but we would be better off not using Greek words like *logos* and *rhema*.

In the conclusion, we'll consider some images that may more accurately reflect the biblical words used to describe such processes, perhaps a better way of explaining how it is that God seems to graciously highlight things to us in his Word, the Bible. How the Spirit reminds us of things we've read when we need them, *and* how he can break into our and others' lives by giving us a *revelation*, i.e. a dream, vision or a trance, or some direct word we may later end up sharing with others.

None of us is immune to getting it wrong, mishearing something we think God has promised us, whether we call it a *rhema* word or not. We cannot take something God has said to someone else and take it for ourselves if God has not made that clear to us. Unless it's a general principle in the Bible, if we a take a word God has highlighted to us and make it a general word or principle, we will get into trouble. This is what Farah was trying to achieve using his general vs specific, *logos* vs *rhema* argument. And as he clearly points out, there are things we'll never understand this side of eternity: some people do not get healed, and it's not their fault, it's often not a lack of faith.

It's why Lamentations (a national trauma) and Job (a personal trauma) are in the Bible for us to help us slowly build a theology of suffering which involves acknowledging mystery and unanswered questions, as well as a theology of healing. If there is no suffering now, then we don't need Job or Lamentations, or any other verses that clearly speak of suffering, as well as accounts of sick people not being healed. For example, Paul left Trophimus 'sick' or 'weak' in Miletus (2 Timothy 4:20) with no suggestion of a lack of faith on Paul or Trophimus' part. The same word for sick or weak is used many times in the gospel to refer to sick people (Matthew 10:8; Mark 6:56; Luke 4:40; John 4:46 – which as we've seen Jesus healed with a 'logos'). As with these other people, Trophimus was definitely unwell; thus, he could not travel with Paul.

At the same time, some of us also need to see far more examples of healing in practice, i.e. the kingdom of God being manifested in the form of miracles such as gifts of healing. Having a theology that includes physical healing today is one thing; seeing it in practice is another (1 Corinthians 12:9). The truth is we need both: doctrine *and* experience.

When I first heard the *logos-rhema* teaching it seemed to smell a bit Barth-like, theologian Karl Barth (1886-1968), to be precise. As well as the good things Barth wrote and did, he believed that the Bible itself was *not* revelation, not *itself* the Word of God: 'When divine revelation meets us and we respond in faith and obedience, the Bible *becomes* the Word of God' (my emphasis);[10] 'The Bible is God's Word so far as God lets it be his Word'.[11]

In other words, you need revelation *for it to become the word of God to you*, something alive. But the Bible *is* the Word of God, God's special revelation, his inspired Word (as opposed to general revelation, God revealing himself through creation – Romans 1:20). It's alive and inerrant in it's original writings. Yes, we need the Holy's

Spirit's light (illumination) in order to understand it, but it does *not* become the word of God as we read it; neither does *logos* become *rhema*[12] which is where we can get into trouble. As we've seen, *logos*, word, has all sorts of uses in the Bible.

CHAPTER 5

Confusion over proverbs

Farah also mentions the misuse of the biblical proverbs, taking them as promises in every situation, of people using them to defend 'word of faith' teaching. And he's spot on. But ironically, here again the logos-rhema tool can be used to distort things and create rules and spiritual laws that apply in all situations. 'Hardly Farah's fault' someone might argue. But like I say, in all this it might be better distinguishing between teaching (for which we need illumination as we engage our intellect in studying or hearing or recalling Scripture) and revelation; the difference between using a knife and fork and using a pick/plectrum to play a guitar (like a musician 'receiving' a song).

For instance, preacher X claims that's he's had a *rhema* word about some proverb and then proceeds to turn it into a law, a now word he's received, and something for everyone to get hold of. 'God gave me the key to this verse! It came alive to me!' It can then become a rule, a promise for all times and situations, a spiritual 'cause and effect' law. But the proverbs are not promises true for every person and circumstance – they are principles that are situation-specific. They are proverbial wisdom, maxims about how life works, wisdom for the people of God about how to live, and which ultimately point us to Christ, the Wisdom of God, who calls out to us. It is *Him* we should fear (Proverbs chapters 1 and 8).

God will sometimes highlight a proverb (as he does in illuminating other verses or passages to us, as we've seen), explaining something that has happened in a situation we're in, i.e. a life-principle at work. But they are not true in every situation (i.e. not promises). For example, it's generally true that 'all hard work brings a profit' (14:23), but that's not true in every situation, it's not a promise for every circumstance. For example, you've worked hard and a world-wide pandemic wipes out your business, or someone steals your money, or your farm you've worked hard on gets flooded.

To emphasis the nature of how proverbs work, a superb example is Proverbs 26 verses 4 & 5 – back to back verses which contradict each other. Try taking them as promises at the same time! They underline the same point: it depends on the circumstances, in this case the particular situation and which particular fool you are dealing with. If you want a really helpful little book on Proverbs and how they work, grab a copy of *How to Read Proverbs* by Tremper Longman III.

CHAPTER 6

Does it matter?

As mentioned, for some in the charismatic wing of the Church who know their Bibles the logos-rhema tool does not present a problem; they have not turned it into a doctrine. They may find it helpful for distinguishing between those times a specific word in Scripture is highlighted to them or brought to mind by the Spirit just when they need it. They may feel that any disagreement over the whole logos-rhema thing is splitting hairs, arguing over mere words (semantics). They can use it as a tool and not get into any bother. But as one Pentecostal pastor friend told me, 'It's an area where cliché can turn into lazy theology which in turn can turn into poor praxis' (custom or tradition).

By using *logos* to refer to the written word of God, the Scriptures, there is a danger in some circles, of inadvertently downgrading the Bible to a dead document that needs 'a revelation' or a *rhema* moment or word for it to become alive or inspired. *Logos* becomes limited to the written word, and *rhema* lifted up to mean the inspired, spoken word. But we've seen that the use of these two words in the Bible do not support this idea. And besides, the Scriptures are 'breathed out', i.e. inspired by God! (2 Timothy 3:16). And Jesus said we are to come to him, the writings are supposed to lead us to him (John 5:37-40).

The written word of God

The word most commonly used in the New Testament to refer to the written word of God, is 'graphe' (pronounced 'grah-fay') and it means 'sacred writing' or 'scripture'. Less commonly used is 'gramma' meaning 'letter' or 'document' e.g. 'Take your *bill*' (Luke 16:6). Both come from the Greek verb 'grapho' meaning 'to write', as in Matthew 4:4, 'It is written'; or when the Roman soldiers who crucified Jesus took the 'written' sign, 'The is Jesus, the King of the Jews' (Matthew 27:37). Paul refers to the Scriptures as the sacred 'writings', the holy Scriptures, the Old Testament that Timothy had known since childhood (2 timothy 3:15).

Every graphe (Scripture) is God-breathed and is useful for *teaching* etc' (2 Timothy 3:16 – my emphasis to underline the fact again that *teaching* is directly connected with Scripture, while prophecy etc is directly connected with first receiving a *revelation*). Interestingly, in 2 Timothy 4:2 where it says, 'Preach the word', it's not *graphe* that is used but *logos*. Putting it in context of what's come before it, that 'word' is the message about Christ, the message of salvation *that we get wisdom about from God's breathed-out graphe, the Scriptures.* Which is actually central. Using the Bible, the written word of God, without looking and pointing responsibly, in context, to Jesus the Living Word is using it for something other than which God commanded. As should be obvious, that's a deadly serious matter.

What if God were to summon you or me tonight and ask, 'Explain to me why you used my Word to preach and teach on things without focusing on my Son?' The priority is the Master, not money; servanthood, not spelling out principles for 'success.'

The word of faith

The context of Romans 10:5-18 (especially verse 8 'the word of faith, which we preach') is a righteousness that is by faith, not by Jewish law. The Jews needed to hear the message about Christ, which is why they needed preachers, which is why preachers like Paul and others needed to be sent. Beautiful feet bringing the good news. Faith did not come, does not come, by law or works, but by hearing the word, the *rhema* of Christ. But the Jews were stubborn (10v21). The passage is littered with not only *rhema* but direct quotes from the Old Testament.

While a different book of the Bible, when we compare it for a moment with Paul's emphasis on preaching the good news in 2 Timothy 4:2 where he uses *logos*, the surrounding and especially the immediate context is about Scripture. My point is that in both passages *rhema* and *logos* are used in connection with Scripture and the importance of preaching so that people will be saved or instructed in the faith. Timothy was to do the work of an evangelist (2 Timothy 4:5).

The logos / rhema of God endures for ever. It's a case of both-and, not either-or.

To recap

Terms (the words and phrases we use to explain things) can become important. God can and does highlight things to us in his word (the Scriptures). We see the tremendous example of our Lord combating Satan with specific words of Scripture (Luke 4, Matthew 4). All believers will have experienced some verse or other really sticking out to them, of God underlining something. 'God really spoke to me!' we say. Amazing! Yet if we are reading or listening to the Bible or sound preaching, *then God is also speaking to us right there and then, i.e. now.* It's not that the Scriptures are stale and need freshening up, or that *logos* needs to become the *rhema* for us. It's more than we need light, illumination, to be given understanding.

Using another illustration for a moment, if the Word of God means nothing to us, it may mean that our ears need circumcised! Not a matter of the word of God needing to become alive, but for our ears to be opened. Jeremiah 6:10 says, 'To whom can I speak and give warning? Who will listen to me? Their ears are closed so they cannot hear. The word of the LORD is offensive to them; they find no pleasure in it' (Jeremiah 6:10, 'closed'... literally 'uncircumcised ears').

What's happening in these situations is that the Holy Spirit has given us fresh insight and helped us see where and how the written word of God applies to our specific circumstances at that time, whether personal, family, church or society. And it's incredible and encourages us in our faith. A good doctor knows which particular medicine to meet our physical needs; our Father and Heavenly Physician and Creator knows not only that, but also which particular passage of Scripture to meet our *spiritual* needs, for we do not live on bread alone. Good shepherds, i.e. elders/pastors have a good idea of which part of the Holy Scriptures apply to the various pastoral needs they are called to minister to. And then there are the other gifts of that same Holy Spirit to enable the church to be blessed and be a blessing.

To repeat: what we need is the Spirit's *illumination* as we read and search the Scriptures; yes, for God to reveal things to us, but not '*a revelation*' or a '*rhema word*' as such, as that's a different thing.

CONCLUSION

Another, better way of describing the difference

When teaching about the nature of prophecy I've sometimes used the image of a 'microscope' versus a 'telescope' to differentiate between what has been called 'forthtelling' (speaking into a person's situation at that time, like a microscope on something in their life and circumstances) and 'foretelling' (predicting the future, like a telescope looking into the distance). Most prophecy is forthtelling. People have found the illustration helpful.

In the same way, instead of using a *logos* word versus a *rhema* word, here are some images that I've already touched on that:

1. Better reflect the difference between those moments when God's Spirit gives *illumination* as we read or listen to the Bible, or recall some verse; and those times when he provides a *revelation* in the form of a dream or vision or some other clear word.

2. More accurately reflect the use of both the words *illumination* and *revelation* in the biblical contexts we've been discussing.

For *illumination*: the image of a **flashlight** or **torch** or **lightbulb** or a **spotlight:** God shining his light on some Scripture or other, which as we've seen can happen when we're on our own with the Bible, or when the Spirit brings some Scripture to mind just when we need it, or when someone is preaching or bringing a *teaching*.

For a *revelation*: when **a song suddenly comes to us** (think of sitting with a guitar, with plectrum/pick in hand) or when **the curtain is pulled back** (think of a play in a theatre) for us to see something behind the scenes that is happening or is going to happen. This can lead to someone sharing it in the form of a *prophecy*.

A **Spotlight** versus a **Curtain** being drawn back. A **Flashlight** vs a **Song**. Take your pick of pairings. You may be able to think of some other useful images.

Going back to the very first page, our part is picking up our knives and forks, getting into the living word of God, and asking the Holy Spirit to give us *illumination*, fresh insight. And if we are gifted to teach, then to bring a *teaching* as God leads us. **And** also pursuing God for the gifts of his Spirit, especially *prophecy* etc, each utterance for which we first need a *revelation*.

We need both these dynamics for the

health and mission of the Church: more, not less of the Spirit and his gifts. The Lord will surely help us if we ask him.

ABOUT THE AUTHOR

Fraser (M.Div., Denver Seminary) has served in churches in several countries. During that time he has recruited, encouraged and developed a number of younger leaders. Some of his books reflect his continued interest in leadership development, while others are aimed at helping Christians more generally, or those curious about the Christian faith. Fraser and his wife currently live in Scotland and have grown-up children, and several grandchildren.

NOTES

[1] *The Pinnacle of the Temple,* Chuck Farah (*Logos* International, 1979) p 25-29

[2] Pinnacle, p 51

[3] *An Expository Dictionary of New Testament Words.* W.E. Vine (Fleming H. Revell, NJ, 1940), p 230

[4] p 51 (my emphasis)

[5] p 50

[6] p 51

[7] p 50

[8] p 49

[9] p 30

[10] Barth quoted in p98 of volume 1 of *Integrative Theology* by G. Lewis and B. Demarest (Zondervan, 1996)

[11] Evangelical Dictionary of Theology (2nd ed). Edited by Walter Elwell (Baker Academic, 2001)

p820.

[12] *Pinnacle*, p28

Printed in Great Britain
by Amazon

72378521R00041